the homeboy songs

robert
lashley

a division of

**SMALL
DOGGIES
PRESS**

Portland, Oregon

SMALL DOGGIES PRESS
a division of Small Doggies Omnimedia
smalldoggiesomnimedia.com

The Homeboy Songs
poetry by Robert Lashley

SMALL DOGGIES PRESS © 2014
1ST PRINTING.

ISBN 978-0-9848744-7-7

PRINTED IN THE UNITED STATES OF AMERICA
10 · 9 · 8 · 7 · 6 · 5· 4 · 3 · 2 · 1

Small Doggies trade paperback edition, April 2014

PUBLISHED BY SMALL DOGGIES PRESS, PORTLAND, OR.

Small Doggies Press: **WWW.SMALLDOGGIESPRESS.COM**

Edited by *Carrie Seitzinger*.
Cover Art by *Matty Byloos*.
Cover Design by *Matty Byloos & Olivia Croom*.
Interior Layout by *Olivia Croom*.
Author Photo by *David Blair*.
Type set in Sabon & **DAYPOSTERBLACK**

CONTENTS

A PRAYER FOR A HILLTOP EPIPHANY

Tell me, Sister, tell me of the journey
tell me of the northern star.

The organ has nothing
to accompany it but the siren.
The preacher speaks of a light away
from multiple kingdoms of Sodom.
The choir starts up, then stands idly by
for the pews remain still, so still.

Invocations of statues, cities and salt
do nothing but calcify movements.
A Gabriel passes over in invisible currents,
a white flaked seraphim
who took every second born
to touch, taste, and inhale him,
who took and calcified their sacred scenes
and engraved in them
hustler head stones—
memories of pieces, fire, and weight
where the unseen seems to linger ever near.

Tell me, Sister, tell me of the northern star.
The hoo-rider is a crocodile that eats the sun
Ghetto birds give no light in south sound slums
where roughneck beasts reside.

Tell me, tell me of the northern star.
Tell me of the places where dead voices gather
the hill here provides no lake or river
yet everyone seems to go down.

23RD STREET ANTHEM

(OR, HOW TO SURVIVE A CRACK SPOT IN SIX EASY STANZAS!)

Be smart, among the crystal corpse arrival.
Be tough among the fire and fires past.
Expect no peace or mercy, just survival.

Keep swiveled head when all heads blow in vial.
Know, among the ruins, you come last.
Be smart among the crystal corpse arrival.

Give them nothing that you consider vital.
Give them nothing for another blast.
Expect no peace or mercy, just survival.

Ignore their demented whines of petty trial.
Dodge the runs of terror that they cast.
Be smart, among the crystal corpse arrival.

Ignore the lasting horror of the dope boy isle.
Leave its beach of sorrow, madness vast.
Expect no peace or mercy, just survival.

Ignore the dope runs down the concrete aisle.
If you cannot, then fate comes swift and fast.
Be smart, among the crystal corpse arrival.
Expect no peace or mercy, just survival.

STONED SURVIVORS LOVE BALLAD
(AFTER A PREDATOR'S BAPTISM)
(I FLIP A LINE OF HEMINGWAY'S)

This is my heart beyond blood and the body.
This is my body more plentiful than bread.
That is revival, the cities of our scars
        gentrified in potters gardens
but these here are the orchards of my flesh,
your joy, in it's improvised defying light
      is my only definition of space.

That was ritual—orthodoxy—order.
That was the deacon who called to a river
      where water is a conceit of the prodigal.
That was where the calf became a well defined lie
where reality is a synonym of haunt.
Yet this, in the space you classify as paradise
      will be whatever you want and need.
The renewal of my mind is transformed by your navel.
The gospel of your space is as simple and complex
      as winter, summer, or spring.

That was testimony: darkness made word.
That was benediction as a metaphor for the graveyards.
Boils and locusts more visible than real
      pass my blood by the Marriot door,
yet Eros is a verb of life in touches and twists
how love, Here. This is my body.
      Remember it as you wish.

POP'S LAST RELAPSE

(WITH A NOD TO STEVENS AND A SNARL AT POUND)

On Sunday, he is still not here.
Absence becomes a Frigidaire's
moonlit reflection in Windex.
apologies are half notes in the post it's between
his bar rack, desk, and floor
 exes,
        "one nighters,"
explanations to mother
                        defensive odes
  that stopped when the subject
  turned concrete and directly to himself.

Tonight, the muses are tired.
The tip of his pen felt like a jail
and he has sung of that song in a glass.
Tonight, find that bar and take his wallet
for hunger has a song beyond night socials.
The corner is not the tomb of Orpheus
but the block where this drunk nigga lay.

John Henry told his bartender,
Well a drink ain't nothing but a drink.
But before I let this life beat my butt
ima die not knowin' how to think
ima die not knowin' how to think.

ST. TERESA OF THE SECTION 8 PENITENT, 1985

(OR, WHY MOM PLAYED TINA TURNER WHEN DAD WENT NUTS)

(WITH A NOD TO ST. THERESA'S PRAYER)

The door bell rings,
then whole locks shake.
Yet she still plays the record
alone and in the dark
upon layers upon layers
of blackness.
> *Save us, St. Theresa*

Sirens ring. Screams are too much.
The rhythm of nation time
is too settled in our bones.
The cities that sent us
to an exile in vouchers
clash among the railing
> *Save us, St. Theresa*

the night molds into a door kick
memory paints in landscapes that shift
to the sound of the niggard outside
to peace be within your 45s and sides
for the side of the door seems fragile
to dreams we piece and scramble to remember.
May you not forget through the crashes
> *Why you motherfuckers fucking
> with my mom?
> She the one that called you?*

Scorched terrain litters the recollection.
Foundations, roots, and underpinnings
reduced to a bloodstained earth;
a sacrifice, in crimson and peal,
to the glories of their nations.

"You don't understand the meaning of the black man POW! POW!"
"You don't understand your white family's pain WHOP! BANG!"
"You don't understand our mind and motivation ZING! POW!"

So they beat it straight out her brain.

"come, let us sacrifice the traitor and her half-breeds
come, let us burn them in drum circles of brotherhood
come, come let us worship our gods,
let us kneel and pray at the foot of our sacred symbols
come, let's go back, go back to our sacred tribes"
"burn baby burn"
"burn nigger lover burn"
"burn baby burn"
"burn nigger lover burn"

Save us, Soul St. Teresa,
from the sacred fire.

ELEGY FOR A STICK UP KID

(THE LAST TIME I SAW MELVIN)

That was your watch—your shirt—your starter jacket.
That was the broach of your grandmother's chain
full of old filtered metals taken at the court
you will never hang with him at, (never again)
those trinkets turned symbols and faded
out jewels that could and could never be sold.
That was his arms, his hands and his fingers
that waved his gun at you in the cold
that winter night, waved as his arm wavered
as the rain shrunk his jersey into a sharp
red fitted skeleton. These are his cheekbones
his pimples, blackheads, the scars from that
rock new enough to be alive, "*Bobby*
you have to keep the procession going."

THE GANG HOUSE GARDEN THIEF'S LOVE BALLAD

For your garden, I will find you hot corner petals.
I will put them in my crown royal bag.
I will search past the weeds—the thickets—the nettles
—search past the Suckas and their impossible tags
and share with you my world in stems and colors
beyond reds and blues (those handkerchief flags).
I will give you my lavenders beyond the hard metals
in 45s, concrete, and faded doo rags
for your love creates me, and love never settles
for environment, so I work. I'll pick them. I'll snag.
For your garden, I will find you hot corner petals.
I will put them in my crown royal bag.

FUNERAL BLUES FOR WHITNEY

(AFTER AUDEN'S "IN MEMORY OF W.B YEATS")

I.

On the day you found what we were missing
us skinny, hungry, thugged out
young boys
stopped dead in front of the boom-box.
Runs were froze. Crap Games almost deserted.
Hood niggas disfigured by public statutes
were transformed by the sound waves
of you back in the day.
On you and your instrument, we young thugs agreed
you were wonderful back in the day.
And far from our projects
little homies dreamed you in evergreen forests
ghetto nerds were transfixed by radio plays
scattered over a thousand stations
scattered—squared—to a thousand more affections
immediately and all at once,
immediately, every time
we heard you and called ourselves
to be better than we were.
Immediately, as we dreamed to be
something grand if not grandiose
if only to win your heart.
If only then, we would scheme up some shit
to unearth the sword from our gravel stones

and win—win you—
and live happily in your kingdom
but the magic dust ate you alive.

II.

Earth, receive a troubled guest.
Whitney Houston is laid to rest.
Let this Newark vessel lie
emptied of our dreams.

For in the nightmare of the dark
all the masks we had of your majesty
ate your face, all our refusals
to look into your blackness
have blinded and scarred our eyes.
Have turned to brown ash
all our crystal strewn pedestals
in a parable of genius and dust.

And now you hang in memory over us
our lady of chemical and too human sorrows
trapped eternally in a crystal cage
only free in the shadow of Sirius,
only free in fleeting notes and electrons
of youth, love and limitless potential

before yours turned slow to a curse.

CHUNKYBROTHERLOVEPOEM

For you, I, an unwashed pear.
I peel all my masks—
synthetic and temporary—
then offer any or all
for want of comfort
desirable and clean.

I spread my sections below
and beneath you,
lay bare as an array
of walls and canvases,
lay, in the seconds
and minutes you want
as a space for your imagination.

Spin me. Spin me.
My globes are yours, love.
My circumference is a land
that centers on your presence
that seasons around your moods
and your movement
in the times you feel a need.

"NO OFFICER, UNCLE WILLIE DIDN'T BREAK THAT HYDRANT, IT CAME OFF BY THE MIRACLE OF JESUS!"

The benevolence of city watercolors.
It softens the shapes
and torrent kissed figures
in pavement turned a furnace by July.

Beside her, the young blood
takes off his church suit.
Beside him, the sister
in the wide pheasant hat
starts to sway around the water's straight line.
Beside them, crowds
from the neighborhood pick up game
gather by and by the new river.

"The water is wide, but we will get over.
This furnace ain't nothing but a short stop in time
ain't nothing but a moment, so now lets get wet.

We will get over, the water is wide."

SONG FOR THE EX-OG BIRD RESCUE MAN

Blood is the color that mixes late September.
It tints the concrete of a late sunset mass
and a mass of errant black birds.
> *The OG in white will take them.*

It is on the wings of those beat and broke in migrations,
those caught up in gun wounds and rickety power structures
those caught in aromas, poisons and toxicants
allusive until they fell.
> *The OG in white will bring them home.*

Allusive is the errant gangsta disciple
as he washes his pavement of red.
Allusive is his second act with body bags
> *Lord, I'll go sweeping through the city, oh my lord*
> *where my niggas have rolled—rolled before...*

At dusk, home goings are everywhere.
Agony moves through the Anglican storefront.
Agony lies still in the gravel.
At dusk, the OG finds place after place
to clean and give proper burials
> *I will stand someday by— By the river.*
> *Won't be back from this block—No damn more...*
> > *The OG in white will take them.*
> > *The OG in white will bring them home.*

TO THE HOMEBOYS WHO RIDE BIKES PAST THE DOPE HOUSES ON STATE STREET, 2008

Although the block is hot, there is no light.
Young ones make moves, but seldom in the sun.
No birds, but bird men stalking all in sight.
No needles, but to all, the damage done.

The young ones move among this trap bazaar,
among a maddening crowd of chemical means.
Among the rich and poor, the hopeless, the bizarre
leeches yearning to trip the dark obscene.

They move among these dens of toxic sprawl,
commerce markets of pieces, weight, and heft
and those who give to no one, yet take all
'til there's absolutely nothing to take left.

Speak on this block, young ones, but speak it clear
But ride on first. There are no children should be here.

DID YOU KNOW WHAT IT MEANT TO BE WITH A BLOOD GIRL

I.

When she laughed, all sound was hers indirectly.
Patterns and cadences formed their own imprint
        that congealed to a need when she was gone?
Measures and movements spun around her Stacy Adams'—
        her hot tracks and polyester.

When she laughed, definitions of humor and gaiety
filed and dissolved to terms around us.
They submitted to her snorts, chuckles and undulations.
They chortled to the absurdity
        of touch, taste and sense
made light by the tip of her tickle fights.

When she laughed, lord nothing else mattered.
Nothing else mattered but her shoulder beside me,
the transfer of brevity and unseen hood light
        that split wide the anxieties of my soul.

II.

Oh, to be asleep with her. Slow. Vibrant.
Sedate, yet alive, so alive.

To be meshed in all the hours
of the nights we spent together.
To be next to her shapes and traces.
To be the face that meets her faces
by the mattress on the floor

To know (or want to know) nothing but her
nothing but all we held between each other
nothing but the hours that lasted like minutes
when BANG BANG BANG BANG...

Hide! Her cousin's a Piru!
A low-cold-blooded-set-tripping-Motherfucker
who brags he's the last one left.

The light in the morning,
to our sense and our senses,
seems so close to death.

GANGBANGER BAPTISM, 1992

They are brought forth, the calf promptly fed,
in trays and painted plates of gold,
in their Sunday best, their carpet rolled
for those who snatched dowry, who left them, who fled.
And they anoint their feet holy, then body, then head
and wash clean their robes of red and of blue.
And the sons who are wary, the daughters who knew
the sins of inheritance, the theft of their bread,
sit outcast in meeting place, outcast in the pew
set forth from the baptized, the sorrowed, the few
beset by the forgiven, and the old story told,
sought a grace, and found only dread.

BLUES FOR BIG MOMMA

I.

You are our pillar, Big Momma.
You are our treasure, Big Momma.
You are the backbone of our community, Big Momma.
You are our rock, Big Momma.

You are being treated like an inanimate object
as you slave over the church stove, Big Momma.
You grab your hands in agony
as you cook all the food
for the Sunday church picnic, Big Momma.
You try not to cry
as you ice the same hands
that were mauled by that cotton plant
with thorns as sharp as knives, Big Momma.
You stir the greens
and try to forget the memory
of looking at the Georgia red clay
and wondering if it got that way
because of our blood, Big Momma.

II.

You done fucked up the food, Big Momma.

You done never get the food right, Big Momma.
You ain't cooked a good piece of chicken since '88, Big
Momma.
You messin' up, Big Momma.

You are trying to block out the memories
of the meals you cooked for the deacons,
the deacons' fathers and their fathers after that
without them ever getting you
as much as a glass of water, Big Momma.
You yearn for the day
when someone would unshoulder your burden,
when someone would tell you
thank you, Big Momma
bless you, Big Momma
you have done enough, Big Momma
you can rest now, Big Momma
rest now, Big Momma.

III.

You ain't never gave me no play, Big Momma.
You hasslin' me about support, Big Momma.
You ain't supportive of the black man, Big Momma.
You ain't my color or size no way, Big Momma.
You are trying to block the memory
of the man who left you
forty years ago
with child and without notice, Big Momma.
You are wondering if there ever was

a Black is Beautiful movement
then why didn't anyone tell you, Big Momma.
That your lips were beautiful
that your body was beautiful
that your shape was beautiful
that your skin was beautiful
that your hair was beautiful
that you were so much more than the cooking brood mare
that we deemed you to be, Big Momma.

IV.

You ignore them boys, Big Momma.
It's just a song, Big Momma.
So what if it is about rape, Big Momma.
You leave them boys alone, Big Momma.
You are trying to forget the frat boys
who came to the plantation
to take what was left of your innocence, Big Momma.
You are trying to forget that feeling
that you would have hanged yourself on a tree
if you stayed any longer, Big Momma.
That you couldn't take one more, Big Momma.
Not one more, Big Momma.
You remember seeing Joan Crawford
being touched by Montgomery Clift at the picture show
and dreamed of a time when a man would touch you
like that, Big Momma.
You feel you have finally woke up in this kitchen
with the realization that dreams are as worthless
as they seem, Big Momma.

V.

Where are you going, Big Momma.
You done lost your mind, Big Momma.
Why are you leaving, Big Momma.
You have a low parson, Big Momma.
You have left the church, Big Momma.
You are going to hell, Big Momma.

Then run, Big Momma.
You have been sinned against Big Momma.
If you have a low parson
* then your parson is worthless, Big Momma.*
If you have left the church,
* then the church has long left you, Big Momma.*
If you are going to hell
* then there is no heaven, Big Momma.*
So if they throw you out
* then run, Big Momma.*
Make this your great getting up morning, Big Momma.
Fare thee well, fare thee well, Big Momma.
You have searched high low for the River Jordan
* and not found it on this bitter earth, Big Momma.*
Find your own River Jordan, Big Momma.
Make your own way to the land, Big Momma.
For you will not view the host in white,
* the host in white will view you, Big Momma.*
You will not come up with every nation
* very nation will come up with you, Big Momma.*
For you will not cook for the welcome table
* the welcome table will come and feed you, Big Momma*

and on that day the saints will come to tell you
thank you, Big Momma
bless you, Big Momma
you have done enough, Big Momma
you can rest now, Big Momma
rest now, Big Momma.

AMERICAN LAKE, AFTER SKIPPING
CHURCH CURFEW, 3AM
(OR, WHY I SPENT ALL MY CRAPS MONEY AT
TACOMA BOYS PRODUCE)

It was the way she ate a peach.
My fault lines would move with every bite.
The Sunday moon would stop and sketch her
but could never create the conscience of her body,
could never duplicate 🔥 in scenes or landscapes
the way she chewed and swam.

It was how everything seemed to refract around her:
shorelines dulled and faded to background,
currents rose and fell to the movements of her mouth
and the kinetic charge of her leg hair.

When she ate, risk was only a number,
gain the materials of paper and alloy,
peace a place that could pass no understanding
till it understood her hunger.
When she ate, no spirit could move rock or sea
like her when she was satisfied.

NO COUNTRY FOR AN OLD THUG

(AFTER YEATS'S "SAILING TO BYZANTIUM")

I. The Homie Pours His Liquor

An aged homie is but a paltry thing.
A tattered jersey, chain and doo rag.
A tattered life plays shadow tag
in bombed out streets and buildings.
Sages standing in holy corners
laugh as he grinds through the metal of his teeth,
laugh as his slobber coats him a sheath
of crimson.
        Interpreted by the crowds
and the early morning traffic
he is a billboard,
            a mark,
something to part from and gaze away.
Windows close. Patrons look away
and restaurateurs shudder at him.
Pawn shop owners re-shift their locks.
Yet he remains—jersey, overcoat, and socks
              and screams

"This is for my homies."

II. The Homie Gets Robbed

The boys here on hillside are to become thugs
and the old thug, now, has his bottle.
They will their young and unsteady legs
to perform their rite and ritual.
They push and claim this is their spot.
They push and brag of loot they got
then punch him in the throat.
A sense of bravado seems to revolt
   one
but his cliff gets closer and closer,
an end, a passage in forcible transfer
of youth to age in the grass.
And the young blood counts cash
and as the old one sips booze,
he mutters
             "I was you once."

III. "Lil Homie 'Ganst the Wall

   Hey, Can't You Hear Your Mama Call"

Yet he cannot receive their slender thread.
Though their memory in ice, it has no need
for crip walks frozen in permanence.
Yet he won't come. He can't come,
though the projects on their tables
are not feasts but covers
they knit from his old glad rags,

their sewn together elegies
in old socks and long shorts,
a coda, made into a wool winter coat
pieced in haste over his distance
and end in the snow pile.

They make their patterns in fury.
They create worlds in fabric to seem
more real than the material seen
in his falls and Sunday
benders. Yet in the cold
the dope head thug cannot receive
their slender thread.

IV......

This is no country for an old thug.
The young are in one another's graves.
The birds in no trees seem empty
in the shine of gentrified building.
Those dying generations
aside Quiznos and Subways
are marked alive in set trips
and mad dog.

IF A BLACK BIRD MOVES AS A COP GRABS YOUR CROTCH, DOES IT REALLY MAKE A SOUND?

The black birds move—first down then up.
They move without asking them where or why
the unseen brings comfort only in

decoration of flight—past the rim—the top
of the backboard—above the stripes that lie
on the side of his shoulders as he lines

you to get a collar. They move through
the blue and the space in the sky without
halt or identification. They move

to a new home through fluff doors of white
without arrested, inorganic
distractions. They move to a range free from

gunshot or tracker away from city blocks—
Free, they move away: flight is their cycle.
Their order and form—their proper procedure

their cover in the day as imagination
and movement lay frightful, so frightful below.

LAMENT FOR MY BOYS WHO PLAYED HOOP ON 23RD

Through the thicket
that is now the court,
I see them move in triplicate
                    Bobby—Milton
Melvin—and Derek.

Small but fast—
fluid—synergistic
four units of one whole.

Milton on point, Derek on first option,
Melvin on post, and Bobby with the midrange—
lord, he has a midrange—

Ricky Pierce midrange—Eddie Johnson
midrange—not-flashy-
but-gets-respect-from-every-

motherfucker-on-the-court
midrange.
He's five foot nothing with a head

as big as the ball but he has
a spot because
he has a midrange.

Through the weeds,
I see flashes of summer runs past,
us down the court—graceful—in packs

disparate yet together. *Derek takes*
the ball to the front, then passes

it to Melvin who shakes two
defenders then takes it to
the paint who throws it back to Milton

who throws it back to Melvin
on the key—then finds
Bobby—wide open—

Smooth—Silky
fifteen feet from the left side—
he shoots
              and they're gone.
Dope house to jailhouse
to nuthouse to the hearse.
The low toned swish
of an invisible hoop, a whistle

past so many graveyards.

FUNERAL MOURNER'S TAG

In his beginning was a wall,
a slab of brick—mortar—
industry concrete reformed to formlessness
by the miracle of Krylon;
reformed by a line
that almost moves itself
in layers, tags and accents.
Spray-painted breaths
of grass and the earth
are signatured
for his homeboy's memorial.

In layers, his boy
is there then away
from him, a shadow
in his oaks, the equation
in his numbers
and letters that split
and construct meaning.

Sirens will ring soon.
Light will be blinding artifice.
Yet the homeboy will still search
for his homie's face
in abstractions over clarity
over abstractions. Art history

will soon be ivory soap here,
yet tonight is not for product
but process.

GENTRIFICATION

The bulldozer took all and then it took nothing;
it took all that most could stand to see.
It took all that was dead and that was scarcely living.
Took dungeons of thugs, but left what they shook.
Took all but the memories, and those that could look
and those who had been there, but could never be
at this progress, this rebuild, this new construct siding,
this pavement of history, but never for me.
The bulldozer took all and then it took nothing;
it took all that most could stand to see.

TO DEREK, WHO PULLED A PISTOL ON ME THE LAST TIME I SAW HIM

Your face is a mask overlooking the chamber.
Steel upon steel, fibers
twined and balled into a ribbing
beyond madness.

It was the memory that triggered you,
My reminiscence that drove you mad
my good talking that made you touch
me in the head with it
as intimate as the way you threw it from the key
or passed me your auntie's red Kool-Aid
or laid me this ground work once
in short grounded words:
"Be quiet. Be aware. Keep your eyes open.
Don't let niggas get you.
Don't let 'em fuck with your mind."

Yet I, a visitor now,
        was fucking with yours.

"Ease up with the mouth, nigga
Why the fuck are you talking all happy and shit?
Why the fuck are you back here?"

ANTI-ELEGY

Your son shermed to death in makeshift car.
His loss was felt (but yours was felt the more).
Don't be a dad tonight, go to the bar.

His momma cries and prays to morning star.
She prays now that he reach celestial shore.
Your son, shermed to death in makeshift car.

Forgive us for not getting who you are,
but please forgive away from worship door.
Don't be a dad tonight, go to the bar.

A girlfriend mourns a body burned to char,
embalmed in a butane threshing floor.
Your son, shermed to death in makeshift car.

A whole church grieves in ways you feel afar
but you don't know the one they're grieving for.
Don't be a dad tonight, go to the bar.

Save the crying rap for the ripple jar,
the only brown thing you showed feeling for.
Your son, shermed to death in makeshift car.
Don't be a dad tonight, go to the bar.

THIRTEEN WAYS OF LOOKING AT A MOTHERFUCKER AT THE CLUB

(AFTER WALLACE STEVENS—MWAHAHAHAHA!)

I.

Among twenty bros at the club
the only thing moving toward my cousin
was the eye of the motherfucker.

II.

I was of three minds
like the IQ
of the motherfucker at the club.

III.

The motherfucker at the club
whirled in the autumn wind.
It was a small part of some corny bro dance.

IV.

A Maxim magazine and Axe body spray
are one.
A Maxim magazine, Axe body spray

and a motherfucker at the club
are one.

V.

I do not know which to prefer,
the time when the motherfucker at the club
says to my cousin
"Girl, I want to sop you up like a biscuit."
or
Girl, you look good enough to season greens with."
or
"Girl, if your left leg is Christmas, and your right leg
is New Years, can I visit you
between the holidays?"

VI.

Bros filled the window with
barbaric glasses of liquor
a rapper drank on BET.
The motherfucker at the club
drank them, to and fro
an indecipherable case.

VII.

Oh thin bros of Seattle,

why do you imagine that you
could put Rohypnol in my cousin's drink?
Do you not know my juvenile assault record
when you walk the feet
of young lady around me?

VIII.

I know Noble accents
and lucid, inescapable rhythms,
but I know too
that if the motherfucker at the club
gives her that drink, I will catch a case.

IX.

When the motherfucker at the club
flew out the window,
it marked the many circles of black around his eye.

X.

At the sight of the motherfucker at the club
flying outside the window,
a bawl of euphony cried out
What did I tell you? What the fuck did I tell you?
If you put your hands on my cousin again
I will cut the bacon off your back and fry it

to your goddamn daddy.
I swear before god, boy,
I'll bust your head to the white meat
and kick you up and down this block
till your ass tore out the frame
And what the rest of your bros looking at?
Which one of your motherfucker's wanna axe
the dentist to get they teeth fixed.
Don't let the smooth tweed fool you!

XI.

The motherfucker at the club ran past downtown
with a busted hand.
Once, a fear pierced him
in that he mistook
someone else
for a person who was driven away.

XII.

The wind is howling.
The motherfucker at the club is somewhere in a corner.

XIII.

Grrrrrrrrr.

MR. JOHNSON TASTES THE DIRT FROM HIS SWEET TOMATO GARDEN

An intimacy—invisible—
yet vivid in movements.
A interchange of earth and the body.
                    Early, my god, without delay,
                    I strain to seek thy face...
In the garden, all agony is sanctified—
made holy—washed clean in the sediments—
the purifying of mud—and the field—
for a moment—redeemed in the spring crop,
the blue gummed meridian of toil and the toiler
the renewal of sweetness and the seasons.
                    My thirsty spirit fades away,
                    without thy cheering grace...
Taste, and what is broken
becomes whole in the roots.
Taste, and all is vivified in the body.

TO MY UNCLES WHO PLAYED DOMINOES

*(AND TO MY UNCLE MOE, WHO DIDN'T COMPLETELY
MAKE IT BACK FROM THE WAR)
(WITH A NOD TO ELIZABETH BISHOP)*

The old soldier fell, but did you see him fly?
In the black of his room, his eyes are shut
stanzas that held him together
have fell to the floor
      C'mon Moe,
       c'mon play a game with us.
Rivers of commissary lunch
hang over his uniform and notebook,
hang over his bar cloth
and the shots that he took
between silences pounded and driven,
between the margins of the delta
and the bone yards that lay
at the feet of his paper and syllables.
      C'mon Moe,
      c'mon play a game with us.
      Yesterday's hurtin, man.
      Don't let it mess with your
mind.
      C'mon, Moe. C'mon and play.

Pow! Come get this ass whipping.
Pow! Get ready for this
Fifteen. Pow! None y'all got nothing
on this twenty five. All y'all niggas
give me some money.

Man, you ain't nothing 'pared to me.
When I was young, I was the baddest thing
in uniform,
young, black, green, and pretty.
Boy you a lie. When I had my outfit
I was smoother than Ollie Matson.
Lord, none a y'all ever told the truth.
When I was sharp, the women used
to call me Moe knew.
Why? Cause every one of them knew Moe.
Yes I was something back then, lord.
Yes I was. Yes I was. You
is something now, man.

WHY UNCLE MILTON WENT OFF ON THE PORTER

Because of the rails on his back.
Because his rocky tops—tacked to them
a hustled away pension—
are unseen Tennessee mountains.
Because variations of screw-ups
at the sight of his pride
spur his movements to the pray.

Fix your uniform, boy.
Don't slouch when you move
I'm too goddamn old to be telling you this.

Because the idea of it's order
still compels him through the pain
in his hands and fists
Because the delicate structures
of his fingers can still list
and lecture the youngblood in job training.

Stand up, but move slow, boy.
Smooth, smooth movements.
Give them nothing but the food, boy.
Nothing but your smile.

Because, he can still time without sight
the rhythms of the chicken plate

and salad tray.
Because his body will still hurt if he doesn't
help out with the port and the porter.
Because fairness and structure
are burnt lies on his back
but order here he can control.

IN THE MORNING, BEFORE UNCLE MOE'S SPECIAL FRIEND HAD TO LEAVE

Through a crack
is never the best place to see her.
Through a crack, their window
is never a mirror. The time they keep
in their invisible hourglass
begins to fade with a car horn
and the deepness of a color
too complex for the letters that form blue.

On their bed sheets
are their moments
that I knew only in pictures.
Black and white photos
of jazz-jointed weekends
that lie over the clothes he fitted her,
lie over their pills,
a triplicate of bottles,
and unfinished projects
on the floor.

**

Stanzas. Jazz songs.
A hem in her grandson's
first communion suit

that—in a fight—he tore.
The button's in the shirt
her husband wore out
when she learned of the secretary
in Denver.
The half smoked reefer
that made her speak of the sea
when he caressed the gray
of her hair.

＊＊

When he fastens her garter belt,
she speaks of their Packard
and the air in another life.

ODE TO A BASEMENT HAIR SALON

The strands are swift, finely woven,
tied together in layer and counter-layer.

The solution holds by column and section,
by the tingle of your scalp
and scald of your skin,
by your evocation of tears
and swift cries of agony
in the finished product and process.

In time, the pain of the hot comb subsides.
In time, the long and natty waves
will be tethered in row after row.
In time, these tears, these layers of sweat
will braid and carry you a crown.

It's OK, baby, I ain't gonna take much longer
ain't trying to hurt you just trying to get it right
it's OK, baby, be still, be still.

HAMBONE AT THE BAR-B-CUE SMOKER

At the head of the line,
and his sodium sky
his spices, salts, and pork fat fry
into uneven December clouds.
   Hambone, Hambone where you been?

The side fryer crackles
Constellations of the side fryer appear, then disappear—
The wind's benign razors straighten a city block
as a well dressed congregation forms.
   Hambone, Hambone where you been?
The procession braces.
They rub their hands in the ice drafts.
They put their palms in and out of their pockets
to cut through the pretense of warm food
in winter: They look and long for him:
the talking drum major
and his flips, pats, and seals.
   Hambone, Hambone where you been?

   All around the world and back again.
   Ham*bone,* **Hambone** *what you do?*
   Fixed you a *sandwich. Eat some food.*

LAMENT FOR A WAFFLE HUT

"The stars are dead. The animals will not look.
We are left alone with our day, and the time is short, and
History to the defeated
May say Alas but cannot help nor pardon."
                                    —W. H. Auden, Spain, 1937

The shack is left dead.
Its walls are torn thin.
The light in her cornbread basilica dims
and the wrecking ball rings
a cacophony.

The shack is left dead.
The landscape's left clear.
Assemblages of the hungry appear
as foundations crumble and set
in the dust.

Cutting boards and pots
are knocked beside the kitchen.
Lost jars of bacon grease
and syrup and juices
mark a toll upon the hill.
Old breads and piece meals
are ground to a gray
as the ball stops
and people keep moving.

The shack is left dead. The people
will not look.
We are left to our morning, and time is short
and waffle cooks, defeated,
may say alas, but cannot help or feed.

A BLOCK PARTY DJ'S LAMENT

Youngblood! Young blood!
We want to dance by the blue light!

Youngblood! Youngblood!
Won't you play us our song!

The boards are faded.
The blue lights of July
are in slices of the outside.

That beam in and accent
your old shadows,
that beam and make distinct

your turntables consumed
by months of dust flecked Sundays.

Past the construction sign
a thug punks a girl across the street

a chain link fence opens—
then closes—then opens again

a passerby in someone else's ride
spits out his bars
of a song of a city
he was far too young to remember

The bass of a jackhammer
and the waltz of a crane
start a gentrified funeral march.

Oh Keisha! Oh Tasha! Oh Niecy! Oh Tinesha!
With your braids, your tights, and your corner born swaggers.
Your hips, your lips, and your tight cropped perms.
Your dimples, scrunchies and sad beautiful eyes
that made me want to give you my world
when you darted then away from me.

Youngblood! Young blood!
We want to dance by the blue light!

Youngblood! Youngblood!
Won't you play us our song!

HOW NOT TO THINK ABOUT SLAVERY
WHILE LISTENING TO THREE 6 MAFIA

(OR, NO, I DON'T THINK IT'S THAT HARD OUT HERE
FOR A PIMP)

Look away from their ice, the glitter and such.
Do not think of cattle, oxen, or pain
for their pictures, though silent, say far too much.

Don't think of their blood, the soul catcher's punch,
the taking of bounty with encrusted chain.
Look away from the ice, the glitter and such.

Don't think of the gentry, the dawg's or the Dutch
nor the color of their dirt, their clay or their grain
for their pictures, though silent, say far too much.

Don't think of their auction, their prod or their touch
their sizing of the breast, testicles, brain.
Look away from the ice, the glitter and such.

Don't think of the bee, the chopping block crutch
and the cut of the day, come shine or come rain
for their pictures, though silent, say far too much.

To think of it all is to think far too much.
To think far too much is to think you're insane.
Look away from their ice, the glitter and such
for their pictures, though silent, say far too much.

BLUES FOR PEACHES

You wanted them there. The bible told him so.
You wanted a mark there of the song he sang.
Why or what for, I will never know.

Who heard your music here (when you had to go)?
The soft sung gospel tones you chimed and rang.
But you wanted them there. The bible told you so

and so I buried them, in a place that doesn't show
or show too much of buildings' Strum and Drang.
It's what you wanted. Why, I will never know.

For I never knew or had the chance to grow
enough to understand your gospel pangs.
But I'll bury them here. The bible told you so.

And now I leave you, my Nicean pilgrim of sorrow.
Lost among the throng to see the Kang'.
Why or what for, I will never know.

Forgive me for my understanding slow.
Forgive me if my distance caused you pain.
You did forgive me. The bible told you so.
Why or what for, I will never know.

11TH AND TACOMA AVENUE, THE MORNING OF PRIDE PARADE, 15 DAYS AFTER JERMAINE SMOKED HIMSELF AWAY

The streets will be full soon.
The sun will show out here
in many shapes and colors.
Love then will exhibit
its unending gift for metaphor,
and the McDonalds will not arch
like your gravestone.

Bodies bright and beautiful
will fill all the streets
in place of your bullies
and tormentors.
Traffic will overflow
with an undefined light
that no parent will put asunder
(though the midnight of your mind
that was cast by your family
will coat every color here
in shadow).

The light that never lit for you
will burn fierce but distant.
The day you never saw
will come, and then go.
The home you so begged for
but never received

Cultural Gentrification

will be here, but now you're away.
Jerusalem will be free (for a day)
from that book
but it will take on the countenance
of your face.

PORTRAIT OF HOMEBOY, AFTER BEING FRISKED BY CRIPS AND THEN LIBRARY POLICE

Your caverns are laid out in trap houses.
Your Traps are in decimal caves.
Youngblood, no things but ideas will save
you from triggers (and the triggers in your bones).

Outside, they are there but they won't go.
Inside, they hinder but they don't know
Blue robed pharaohs have different clothes
but staffs hurt just the same.

Youngblood, the promised land is interior.
Place (and its physicals) bonds a hot fever
that is permanent to all but your sky.
Freedom—right now— is your gift to ask why
and to move first—to home—to shelter
Youngblood, your triggers are a river of sight
       but to stay in them is to die.

THE STROLL: MARCH 13, 1992

(OR, I GO TO SCHOOL WITH HER, POP)

In the vacant lot, the old men sing
yet the stroll is too painful for verse or rhyme.
> *It may be the last time we both play together*
> *maybe the last time, I don't know*

Blooms and gardens are words by concrete.
Blooms where our blood exists.
Extensions are stilled by the threat of magnums
in the blue and black of six.
> *It may be the last time we both sing together*
> *maybe the last time, I don't know*

In the vacant lot, grief lives as itself.
No words or syntax of roses and fields
no smooth or silky playa pastorals
that numb in sound and body,
that paint in brushes that elude all hands
an eternally bloody sky.
> *This may be the last time we all meet together*
> *maybe the last time, I don't know*

In the vacant lot, the old men sing
yet the young are deafened in their garden.
> *One of these morning, won't be long*

> *You'll look for me, a child…*

POPS

"The man on the street is a victim, and a victim is capa-ble of anything."
      —*Robert Lee Lashley, Seattle Post Intelligencer,*
           July 18th, 1990

The bleeding's in the scars that never show,
the seeps and leaks from body and from brain.
Forget, forget more than you'll ever know.

The mind contracts when body starts to grow.
The damage done in place beyond the brain.
The bleeding's in the scars that never show.

Detritus rises in mind high and low,
detritus beyond the white pale of the grain.
Forget, forget more than you'll ever know.

Thrust toward madness, navigate the blow,
the strokes that tore your circulating lanes.
The bleeding's in the scars that never show,

The scorn of the corner! *"You yo daddy's ho.
C'mere nigga, come and give me brain."*
Forget, forget more than you'll ever know.

In demands of secrets, say it isn't so.
Saying not, the way to keep you sane.
The bleeding's in the scars that never show.
Forget, forget more than you'll ever know.

AS HE SEARCHED THINGS TO PAWN
FOR THAT SHIT, BIG MOMMA...

hummed in a key more ancient than Eden,
in a melody beyond reach of thugs
and the grasp of the material world.

The old man ran to the rock
but the rock could not hide him,
though he took every trinket in trying.
He took every heirloom and broke rosary bead
to an altar of a grainy white god.

Above her, ghetto birds
circle and circle each other.
An old man among young men
looks over and over
her records, tapes and eight tracks.
Above her, the snap of a record player cord
skips a beat in her sound.
It will be all over, lord.
It will be all over.
Joy will be in the vacancy of one morning soon.
Above her, the thugs rumble.
The floor becomes something never the same
and music recedes from the rest of her day
and the loss of her roots—
of her dirt and her clay—
becomes deafening.

It will be all over, lord.
It will be all over.
It will be all over someday.

CHURCH CAMP: ROLLING OLD TESTAMENT PAPERS WITH HER

(AFTER FRANK O'HARA'S "HAVING A COKE WITH YOU")

Was so much better than going to Samaria-
Judea-Gideon-Babel-Murta

or pleading the blood at the Kmart altar,

partly because I loved her,
partly because she had the sickle cell,

partly because the deacon read *Black Tail*
in the back pew
and was far less cleaner than she.

The secrecy of our smiles
took off before the sanctuary of dietary laws,

as we rolled up Eziekel's
obsession with her and animal junk.
I looked at her

and would rather have looked at her
than all the books of Moses,

their portraits seemed to have no face
as radiant
as she there, blazed in the grass.

CHURCH CAMP: CONFERENCE ROOM
(WHAT A FRIEND WE HAD IN RAZZLES)

Through light and glass she defines all matter
though nothing of matter will lightly define her,
nothing of matter in the surrogate of Lips

between blood, a bed, and a bowl.
Seeds.
          Sticks. Stems of fathers.
Sorrow burns along with the terror of touch
and smoke alarms lose sound and meaning
in abandoned jesus conference rooms.

Through light and glass, the world is her laurel.
Her holly seeds filtered all light and shadow.
Sorrow is an invisible city of fabrics
from her, and in the world outside.

CHURCH CAMP: IF YOU SEE MY HOMEGIRL, TELL HER THAT YOU SAW ME

I. Before They Kicked Us Out:

The only thing we did was touch.
Our roaches were gone into the aether.
Our stolen boom box was out of power,
and my menagerie of boasts
on Dutch Red ripple
gave way to the crickets and grass
gave way to cuddles and pinky sworn stories
of *David and Biggie! Batheshba and 2pac!*
The serpent and the gold chain gangsta's
feet of bronze, sex and wantonness!
Yet everything I wanted was there;
the red rightness of her curls,

the smell of her air, the warmth
of her inner thighs that made
me take off my ice and jersey.

II. After:

And though days and days I dreamt about her
every ending I had was snatched to the real,
every altered shape and intensified color
ripped clean by the finality of elders,

ripped clean in our nakedness
by the group of our brothers
rejoicing in shame, sin and loss.
And home, I walked that suburb senseless
to try and try and find her.
    Yet the grass stayed straight.

The evergreens wouldn't bend.
Every streak and glimpse of red
would mirror her,
then evaporate to the gray of the concrete
the sound and actual of morning
though nothing but her there seemed real.

SELF PORTRAIT OF HOMEBOY IN THE SUBURBS (THREE HOURS AFTER HIS BOYS BEAT THE CRAP OUT OF HIM)

In your great gettin' up morning they fared you ill.
Their hands inside your tears marked time and memory.
Your half-seen eye: a price for getting by

and getting over to a new Jerusalem called
a dueling corner strip mall. On that morning
the coming of judgment is a blotch over

old forests, and gazed darkly through a Chrysler
the promised land lives in shadow. Stop trying
through the window to see the scenes (now only moulds).
Tints of place and dreams that your friends and teachers told
you of? They taunt you past the slits that are your eyes.

In your great getting up morning, homeboy, goodbyes
will beat on you: the price of your ticket in bruises, blood,
and sweat. Half eyes are full of water and regret.
On that morning, homeboy forget forget forget

MY AUNT'S BACKYARD, AFTER ONE OF POP'S BEAT DOWNS

A slit. An acorn.
After that, a cherry blossom.

After that, definitions
of wood and a blackberry bush

take shape from blotches
and greens.
               As your pupils lift,
the sun is less of an overseer

quick movements and flashes
lose all sense of their danger.

The silence of the grass
takes a comfort

and shape on your face
and on your backside.

The scenery, large and over your head
doesn't swarm or overwhelm.

OLD NEIGHBORHOOD ALTAR CALL TRAPPER KEEPER

(OR, ON THE CORNER OF 19ᵗʰ, NO ONE CAN HEAR YOU FEEL THE SPIRIT)

> *"The palm at the end of the mind,*
> *Beyond the last thought, rises*
> *In the bronze distance."*
>
> —*Wallace Stevens*

A regiment of rain and wind
touches and fades its dissolved out shape,
to a dissolved, cardboard skeleton.
Outside service, it crumbles in your hands

Ink bleeds through angels and outlines
Streams of black and gray
move toward
                Communion
baptism
                Sister Johnson's passage.

Altar call for the lost, for the sick
and **shut in.**
                Keeping memories alive
for the times of our lives
now a clay of soaking Kodak.

And for a moment, their soul claps
are louder than silence,
wavelengths of force, unrestrained

energy are individual,
yet in their spasms of movement
theirs and theirs together.

And for a moment, you are claimed here
but only for a time.
You feel the unseen
in an unforeseeable moment.
You will render and be rendered
in recurrence and congregate
in a union of sound, soul, and step,
but then it stops.

The hand in the hand
is the mother of motion,
Yet in the altar call
the nerd has no home.

MAMA, IT'S OK IF YOU DON'T WANT TO SMILE

Mama, your stomach holds a billon words:
a billion gulps, spits, groans and swallows.
Mama, you don't have to try to hear the birds.

Jagged spasms make external your herds
of interior matter and sorrows.
Mama, your stomach holds a billion words.

By your blood, all my reality is blurred.
My skin holds only in metaphors
Mama, you don't have to try to hear the birds.

The weight you carry, by god it mattered
and matters, but don't carry those burdens
on my account now; those billion words

coded in the language of survivors.
Coded, stoicism cannot coat our traumas.
Mama, you don't have to try to hear the birds.

Coded, the real is a veil over your lips
its form now can only surface in tremors.
Mama, your stomach holds a billon words
(a billion gulps, a billion swallows).
Mama, you don't have to try to hear the birds.

BIG DADDY'S LAMENT FOR BIG MOMMA

"There are times—times, boy—when I dream of death.
Time is a dream, now, of her face in the rain.
These times, boy, I feel I have nothing left.

Time centers around the way that she left
yet time has no way to center this pain.
There are times—times, boy—when I dream of death.

My time is a weight, a burden, a heft
to carry another day—then again—then again.
These times, boy, I feel I have nothing left.

Time saved me from the swinging—those roots—that cliff
yet her branches still bleed now, still bleed in my brain.
There are times—times, boy—when I dream of death.

Time calls it passage? Boy, I call it theft.
In my dreams, the tile is a burning red plain.
In these times, boy, I feel I have nothing left.

Yet I will keep going—I'll wander—I'll drift
to that last meeting place, and I will walk in.
But there are times—times, boy—when I dream of death.
These times, boy, I feel I have nothing left."

BLOOD GANG RITUAL, 1990

By the left end swing and the middle school chalk
the boys took turns with the razor.
Yet-formed cheeks and walnut brown faces
are marked by the rust and the blade—
are marked by mixtures of tears and snot
not yet to leave their face.

Homeboys, Homeboys, where have you gone?
Homeboys, where did you go?
They talk of war marks—gang fights—
—mariners baseball
—of being the king of first period
 after smoking their first fool—
—of running the dope game
 at two after school—
 then marrying Janet Jackson—
—of being soldiers in battlefields or red now—
—but after they eat their jolly ranchers.

Homeboys, Homeboys, where have you gone?
Homeboys, where did you go?

THE LITTLE WHITE DUDE
WITH THE DJ QUIK JHERI CURL

(AFTER WILLIAM CARLOS WILLIAMS'S
"THE RED WHEEL BARROW")

So much depends
upon

a little white dude
with a Dj Quik jheri curl

riding his ten speed
down the block

trying to get his baby momma
at the hair salon

a sandwich.

INSTRUCTIONS TO THE HOMEBOY
ON HOW TO FIX HER HAIR

(WITH A NOD TO NINA SIMONE)

Black is the color
of my true loves weave.
Wave fronts are the rule
of her day job side hustle
Surface work now
is divinest sense
cause she has to get her money,

but be deliberate, homeboy.
Water before the comb.
Activator after water
and a joint in your hand

to keep your ass still
for she has to keep this job.
But the alarm goes off,
the march sun earns
the design of its light
by proxy of her movement,
and suspension of metaphor
around the salt of her neck
start to break
as she leaves the bathtub.

But, boy the clocks beep.
Homeboy, get her hair right.

Nothing is as permanent
as her mini mart silky.
Nothing but the space
between her hair and your chest
should matter
until her weave is seamless.

Fail her, and regret
will make all its definition.
Distance will serve
only qualities of hurt
if you don't place and part
correctly.

Robert Lashley is a semi finalist for the PEN/
Rosenthal fellowship. He has had poems pub-
lished in such journals as *Feminete*, *NAILED*, *No
Regrets*, and *Your Hands, Your Mouth*. His work
was also featured in *Many Trails To The Summit*,
an anthology of Northwest form and Lyric poetry.
To quote James Baldwin, he wants to be an honest
man and a good writer.

In this lurid novel-in-stories, The Motorcycle Gang, a mythic and silent anti-hero whose very presence foretells the coming of the end of the world, descends upon the land. Cast against a dystopian backdrop and set in the near-distant future, the country has devolved into two capital cities: Las Vegas and Detroit. When everyone learns of the end of times, society comes unhinged and anarchy rules the day. But The Motorcycle Gang has a secret that no one else knows...

ROPE

a novel by **Matty Byloos**

$20.00 | 264 pages | 5.5" × 8.5" | softcover | ISBN: 9780984874460

"*ROPE* is totally fascinating. Matty Byloos's precise, crookedly nailed sentences seem to be chiseling the story at large as you read, their signage as fresh and mysterious as the broken branches and footprints of a forest's newly lost visitor. And yet everything is so, so clear. Really beautiful."

—**Dennis Cooper**, author of *The Marbled Swarm* and *God Jr.*

"Matty Byloos's *ROPE* presents an America of the near future that is literally polarized between two inland cities with seemingly irreconcilable values. The time is ripe for a Messiah. Told as a parable, this improbable vision becomes increasingly plausible. Simple and vivid, ROPE is a scary and disarming book..."

—**Chris Kraus**, author of *Summer of Hate* and *Torpor*."

Jacob Rakovan's *The Devil's Radio* broadcasts the elegies of so many, in a voice that lies down with them in their graves, touches their bones, and knows their stories. Cast against a backdrop of Appalachia in exile, Rakovan's collection of poems mines the dark veins of life, love, and death.

The Devil's Radio

poems by **Jacob Rakovan**

$14.95 | 90 pages | 5.5" × 8.5" | softcover | ISBN: 978-0-9848744-4-6

"Urgently tender and elegiac, *The Devil's Radio* not only howls and hurts good, but also sings toward healing with a persistence that is life-affirming and devotional. With language and music that are oak-aged in exile and the deeply felt memory of Appalachia, these poems burn deliciously and relentlessly through the body and mind. Faced with the impossible wreckage of loss, of death after death, of trying to be a good man and father while staring down the thieving threat of graves, Rakovan employs a fairytale-like logic to reinvent elegy, to make sense of the senseless, to knock the grinning face off that 'sonofabitch' death and give the dead and living back their wonder."

—**Stevie Edwards**, author of *Good Grief*

"American ghosts have to make up a song to sing as they weave their flight through our ruins—rural and industrial both. Few people care to listen to the horror and beauty of that chorus. In his debut collection, however, Rakovan tunes into this awesome and terrible ruckus, crafts for us a gothic ballad and rust-blade curse, the psalm plugged into a banged up tweed amp, elegy after elegy, eros, tenderness, fable and praise. After centuries of private wreckage and public forgetting, there is a poet composing something to make sense of it all and the sounds are playing on *The Devil's Radio*."

—**Patrick Rosal**, author of *My American Kundiman* and
Uprock, Headspin, Scramble and Dive

Other titles available from
SMALL DOGGIES PRESS

Into the Dark & Emptying Field is an interrogation of loneliness and its many masks. It explores innocence as the price of knowledge in a host of voices that share an emotional truth. McKibbens offers a monument of understanding for even the bleakest pieces of our human conundrum.

Into the Dark & Emptying Field
poems by **Rachel McKibbens**

$14.95 | 88 pages | 5.5" × 8.5" | softcover | ISBN: 978-0-9848744-3-9

"Hard and as real as the ax blade, the poems in *Into the Dark & Emptying Field* are unapologetically fierce and undeniably gorgeous. Strikingly imaginative and expertly crafted, these necessary poems shine a dubious flashlight on both the menace and the marvel that surrounds us. Otherworldly and at times shockingly brutal, McKibbens' work is both crucial and addictive. "

—Ada Limón

"Rachel McKibbens' work shatters me and my world, then pieces us back together on the page like no other poetry I have ever read, creating a new reality, a self that feels what I cannot feel, sees what I cannot see. These poems are at once dreamscapes and yet as solid and real as stones in my hands, stones I want to press against my chest forever, then hurl back into the infinity of space where words of such beauty and power surely come from."

—Richard Blanco

"The ancient Japanese swordsmiths categorized a sword by how many body parts it could pass through, i.e., a two-neck sword, a three-arm sword...The strongest and deadliest was a four-torso sword. This book is a four-torso sword. You will feel it, hard."

—Jennifer L. Knox

After murdering his elder brother, Marlet must flee the broken town of Victory. With his sword, our low-hung handed hero maneuvers his way through a decrepit southern desert murdering blank-skinned men, being pursued by his illegitimate son, and deceiving those he encounters. All the while, Marlet holds on to his precious memories of Edie, the widowed wife of his brother.

Edie & the Low-Hung Hands
by **Brian Allen Carr**

fiction | $12.95 | 132 pages | 5.5" × 8.5" | softcover | ISBN: 978-0-9848744-2-2

"In turns naturalistic and fantastic, Brian Allen Carr has crafted a truly original tale. This Texas landscape is a mix of country and blues. Larry McMurtry sings Robert Johnson. And then there's the sword."

—**Percival Everett**, author of *Assumption* and *I Am Not Sidney Poitier*

"This book is beautiful. You're going to hell if you don't buy it. I mean that. Carr is a man with magic inside his heat. Read this book and meet a man who will love you forever. Live. Live. Read Carr. You will be alive. FINALLY."

—**Scott McClanahan**, author of *Crapalachia* and *Hill William*

"In *Edie & the Low-Hung Hands*, Carr's alternate world is reminiscent of Denis Johnson's *Fiskadoro*—dreamlike, haunting in its dystopian aura, and fully imagined. The humanity of his characters is never lost, despite the violence and strangeness of their existence."

—**Paula Bomer**, author of *Nine Months* and *Baby and Other Stories*

Carrie Seitzinger's *Fall Ill Medicine* dwells in the body, where memories gather in full color, darkness waits in our deepest feeling trials, and frailties give way to strength. Each poem offers the reader a chance to remember, an opportunity to forget, and a reason to consider the things that make us fragile humans.

Fall Ill Medicine
poems by Carrie Seitzinger

$10.95 | 88 pages | 5.06" × 7.81" | softcover | ISBN: 978-0-9848744-1-5

"In Carrie Seitzinger's collection *Fall Ill Medicine* we are healed. Seitzinger is a doctor of the lyric moment, a humanist of narrative, and had the bedside manner any poet would be lucky to have—that is a verse with truth, mystery, and kinetic energy. As she writes in her poem "Freefall Flight," 'Then I walk to the window and fall out. / And it is beautiful and I am happy.' And so we are lucky to walk into the windows of her poems, and through the fall made beautiful and happy."

—**Matthew Dickman**
author of *All-American Poem & Mayakovsky's Revolver: Poems*

"*Fall Ill Medicine* is a book poems that brings one back to body's story—with a brutal pull soft as moth's wings. There is a love story that exists between objects and silences and ribs. There is a lifestory that makes strength from our frailties. Carrie Seitzinger sings the body home."

—**Lidia Yuknavitch**
author of *The Chronology of Water & Dora: A Headcase*

Other titles available from
SMALL DOGGIES PRESS

J. A. Tyler's *Variations of a Brother War* glimpses at the lives of two brothers, and the girl whom each of them loves. Against the background of the Civil War, these brothers become soldiers, engaging in the most desperate kind of tumultuous love triangle and how it intersects with the astounding tragedy of war. In a world where everything has its own ghost, life is strange and beautiful, even in the midst of conflict.

Variations of a Brother War
by **J. A. Tyler**

poetry | $12.95 | 116 pages | 6" × 9" | softcover | ISBN: 978-0-9848744-0-8

"In Tyler's hands, static concepts become Möbius strips of subversion. This incredible text is a kaleidoscopic set of bifocals: look up and you're in a far-away war, down and you're in a suburban treehouse. Up and you're the victim, down and you're the aggressor. What is so important throughout—what Tyler so remarkably and irrefutably convinces the reader of—is all the ways these binaries are indeed, are inescapably, fused together on the same lens."

—Alissa Nutting
author of *Unclean Jobs for Women & Girls*

"J. A. Tyler's crystalline sentences are a joy to read. In *Variations of a Brother War*, his blocks of dense prose accumulate to form a panoply of cinematic moments. The integrity of this work can be found in its masterful construction and the pathos of its subject watching a story unfold on the pieces of a shattered mirror."

—Ben Mirov
author of *Ghost Machine*

SMALL DOGGIES PRESS

ARTFUL FICTION & POETRY
FOR LOVERS OF THE WRITTEN WORD

———•◦•———

Small Doggies Press supports, defends, and publishes the most beautiful, challenging, and artful prose and poetry that we can find. We believe that the author has all the power, and our job is to create a context within which they, and most importantly their work, can flourish and find the intelligent, curious readership that it deserves.

Small Doggies Press is a division of Small Doggies Omnimedia, LLC, an Oregon. Corp.

VISIT US TODAY:

www.smalldoggiespress.com

CPSIA information can be obtained at www.ICGtesting.com
Printed in the USA
BVOW01s2330160614

356416BV00002B/8/P